PHOENICIANS - MASTERS OF THE SEA: SHIPPING AND TRADING LESSONS FROM HISTORY

By: Mustafa Nejem

CONTENTS

INTRODUCTION

Who could forget the movie "Pirates of the Caribbean"? It's memorable because it features pirates, the sea, ships, thrills, and adventures into unknown lands or seas. Imagine a tale of a civilisation that lived through adventures just as thrilling, if not more so, in the real world. But here's the twist – these mariners weren't thieves; they were brilliant traders, possessing razor-sharp intellect, entrepreneurial prowess, and an unquenchable thirst for exploration. The astounding part? All of this unfolded in the course of history, nearly 4000 years ago. Yes, we're talking about the ancient maritime and trading civilisation known as the Phoenicians.

The Phoenicians were a civilisation that thrived in a region known as the Levant, and they shared similarities with the Canaanite civilisation around 3000 BC. Their legacy in history is defined by their remarkable success as mariners and sea traders around 1200 BC. During this era, they didn't just sail through uncharted waters; they left an indelible mark on the history of maritime exploration.

Later, other renowned ancient civilisations, such as the Greeks, Mesopotamians, and Egyptians, drew upon the inventions and discoveries of the Phoenicians in the realm of sea trade routes and navigation. They adopted innovations like using the North Star for navigation and the trading techniques developed by the Phoenicians. In this manner, we can confidently assert that the Phoenicians were the trailblazers among sea traders and mariners. Therefore, they opened the doors of maritime trade for future generations of mariners, sailors, and traders, leaving a legacy that would shape the course of history.

Moreover, the Phoenicians were exceptional traders and remarkable inventors and innovators. Their shipbuilding expertise was unparalleled in their era, leaving a legacy that continues to astound. For example, the remnants of their shipwrecks scattered across the Mediterranean Ocean are silent testaments to their profound wisdom in shipbuilding and navigation.

Furthermore, ancient historical records bear witness to their prowess as successful merchants and the inventors of Tyrian purple dye, a renowned and coveted product of their time. The Phoenicians' contributions spanned a wide spectrum of achievements, from maritime mastery to groundbreaking innovations and trade, making them a truly remarkable civilisation of their era.

In this era of advanced technology, it's easy to become captivated by the cutting-edge innovations surrounding us. However, it's equally essential to remember and honour our roots, acknowledging the ancient civilisations whose remarkable discoveries and engineering advancements continue to inspire and awe the modern world with their profound wisdom.

While maritime and sea routes may evolve with each passing day, we must recognise that the Phoenicians were the trailblazers who left us a roadmap to follow. Therefore, even in this age of high-tech marvels, modern mariners and shipbuilders still glean a wealth of knowledge and inspiration from the enduring legacy of the Phoenicians. Their contributions remain a testament to the timeless value of history and tradition in shaping the future.

Moreover, the Phoenicians were exceptional traders and remarkable inventors and innovators. Their shipbuilding expertise was unparalleled in their era, leaving a legacy that continues to astound. For example, the remnants of their shipwrecks scattered across the Mediterranean Ocean are silent testaments to their profound wisdom in shipbuilding and navigation.

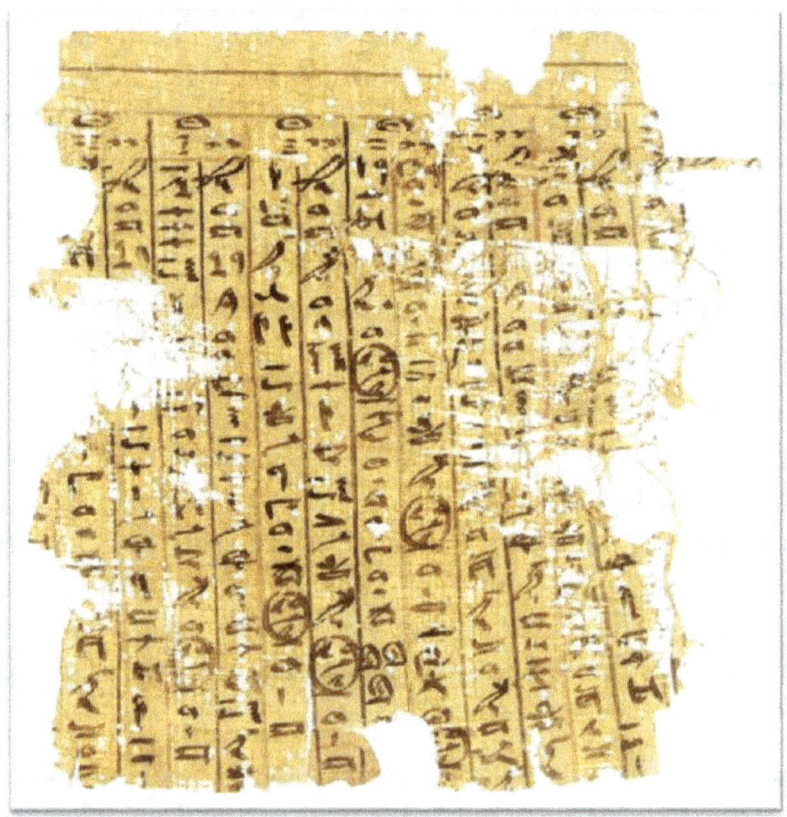

Furthermore, ancient historical records bear witness to their prowess as successful merchants and the inventors of Tyrian purple dye, a renowned and coveted product of their time. The Phoenicians' contributions spanned a wide spectrum of achievements, from maritime mastery to groundbreaking innovations and trade, making them a truly remarkable civilisation of their era.

In this era of advanced technology, it's easy to become captivated by the cutting-edge innovations surrounding us. However, it's equally essential to remember and honour our roots, acknowledging the ancient civilisations whose remarkable discoveries and engineering advancements continue to inspire and awe the modern world with their profound wisdom.

While maritime and sea routes may evolve with each passing day, we must recognise that the Phoenicians were the trailblazers who left us a roadmap to follow. Therefore, even in this age of high-tech marvels, modern mariners and shipbuilders still glean a wealth of knowledge and inspiration from the enduring legacy of the Phoenicians. Their contributions remain a testament to the timeless value of history and tradition in shaping the future.

In this book, we will embark on a profound exploration of the Phoenicians, not merely as a wise ancient civilisation but also as sailors, navigators, shipbuilders, explorers and traders. Our journey will delve deep into their legacy, unravelling the secrets of their maritime prowess and unravelling the mysteries of their trade networks. Along the way, we will discover valuable lessons that we can glean from their experiences and apply to our modern world.

Chapter 1

MASTERING MARITIME EXPERT

Imagine the ferocious sea, rough waves, and the era of 1200 BC. You must be wondering how ships built in this ancient era managed to survive without the aid of advanced technology and techniques. If you know the Phoenicians, you'll not wonder anymore.

The Phoenicians are known for their remarkable craftsmanship in shipbuilding and navigational prowess. The legacy of the Phoenicians, like their namesake phoenix, has created a roadmap to inspire modern mariners, sailors, and sea traders to this day. Additionally, their reputation extended to their skill as sea navigators who fearlessly explored new routes, opening unprecedented trade opportunities through their exceptional navigation prowess.

In this chapter, we will explore how the Phoenicians ruled the sea through their mastery of shipbuilding and navigation.

PHOENICIANS: AS MAGNIFICENT SHIPBUILDERS

Phoenicians were renowned for their shipbuilding and had historical records of making sturdy and sleek ships for various purposes. For example, records like Egyptian, Assyrian, and Hebrew sources vividly describe the Phoenicians as remarkable shipbuilders. They were known for crafting sturdy fishing boats, merchant ships, and formidable warships. Furthermore, ancient sources such as the Bible, Homer's Odyssey, and Herodotus' Histories all make mention of ships that were undeniably products of Phoenician ingenuity.

The trireme stands as the magnum opus of the Phoenicians. This warship, famously used by the Greeks for an extended period, is believed to have been invented by the Phoenicians. It was a vessel consisting of sleek architecture featuring three banks of oars that revolutionised naval warfare and left ancient sailors in awe of its engineering advancements. One can imagine this ship as the fighter jet of the ancient era.

Indeed, the Phoenicians excelled not only in warship construction but also in crafting sailor boats and merchant ships. The Mediterranean Sea itself serves as a testament to the Phoenicians' craftsmanship in shipbuilding. Numerous remains of Phoenician vessel shipwrecks have been discovered in the Mediterranean Sea. Upon close inspection, these ships have left maritime archaeologists in awe of their sturdy design and remarkable engineering advancements.

Many of these sea vessels were constructed using sturdy wood, particularly cedarwood. However, the Phoenicians also employed pine or fir trees for planking in these ships. This strategic choice enhanced their safety as they traversed the vast seas of the world. It underscores their insightful understanding of selecting the right materials for ensuring both the sturdiness and safety of their sea voyages.

According to the research, modern marine archaeologists have undertaken the ambitious task of recreating an 8th-century BC Phoenician trade ship using traditional materials and the supposed techniques employed by the Phoenicians. They took inspiration from shipwrecks found in Tyre, Lebanon, as a model for this reconstruction.

Remarkably, this reconstructed ship has proven its ability to load cargo without becoming stuck in shallow waters. The key to this manoeuvrability lies in the Phoenicians' ingenious use of a shallow draft hull design. This special flat-bottomed design made navigating and manoeuvring through various water conditions considerably easier.

THE LEGACY OF PHOENICIANS AS SHIPBUILDERS

Why and how do modern mariners and shipbuilders use the Phoenicians as an example of shipbuilders?

Nowadays, we have advanced technology and engineering brilliance. People don't just learn from one generation to another; they have universities that teach advanced architectural techniques with the help of cutting-edge robotics technology. So, why should we learn lessons from ancient civilisations like the Phoenicians?

History attests that human beings, whether ancient or modern, have never lacked intelligence. They adapt and drive advancements in their businesses and lives.

INNOVATE TRADITIONAL DESIGN

The Phoenicians learned from existing shipbuilding designs and architecture to their advantage. They grasped the logic that mastering the sea could enable them to dominate world trade, especially since the sea served as the primary route for global travel during their era. This understanding motivated them to adapt and reinvent old designs, transforming ships into powerful tools in their favour.

Modern shipbuilders and mariners should recognise that holding onto our traditions is not hindering advancement. On the contrary, respecting tradition can be the foundation for innovative designs and progress in ways that modern technology alone cannot surpass.

A great example is the discovery of Gozo shipwrecks. In 1987, shipwrecks were discovered in the waters off the Mediterranean island of Gozo. Archaeologists determined that these shipwrecks belonged to Phoenician vessels dating back to around 700 BC. These ships represent a remarkable blend of tradition and innovation, offering compelling evidence of the Phoenicians' commitment to refining traditional technologies while keeping innovation at the forefront of their endeavours.

EFFICIENT AND PRACTICAL DESIGN

Modernity can sometimes lean excessively towards practicality, occasionally overlooking the ideal approach. Conversely, some designers concentrate solely on creating something innovative and unique, inadvertently neglecting the simplicity necessary for the practical use of ships. The Phoenicians, however, managed to strike a balance, never forgetting the importance of both efficiency and practicality in their ship designs.

On one side, their ships were advanced and pleasing to the eye. They were both efficient and practical. To elaborate, they crafted their ships with manoeuvrability, steering balance, and ample cargo space in mind.

A great example of this aspect is Byblos ships. These merchant vessels played a pivotal role in facilitating the expansion of Phoenician trade routes to distant lands. They boasted large cargo capacity, ideal for transporting substantial quantities of trade goods from one country to another.

It is estimated that these ships could carry up to 450 tons of goods while spanning 100 feet. These vessels featured multiple rows of oars and stem-to-stern cables. Modern shipbuilders can draw inspiration from this engineering brilliance to design containers that enhance cargo capacity, ultimately leading to fuel savings and greater efficiency.

IMPORTANCE OF NAVIGATION AND SEAMANSHIP SKILLS IN PHOENICIAN CULTURE

No navigation means no exploration, leading to no trade routes, which means no economic success and leaves no historical traces. The Phoenicians were known in history as successful seafarers and mariners because of their brilliant navigation skills. From the discovery of celestial navigation, such as using Polaris, the North Star, to marking coastal landmarks during their journeys, the Phoenicians made it possible to traverse the seas, thus creating a roadmap for future voyagers like the Greeks and Romans and, later, the Carthaginians and even Irish.

SIGNIFICANCE OF MARITIME TRADE FOR PHOENICIANS

Phoenicians were known for discovering and exploring new trade routes, as the ancient texts explained the hike towards the bygone lands. For example, Herodotus, a Greek historian, wrote about their journey around Africa in 600 BC. While on the other hand, some sources also described their voyage towards Britain and India. It was possible only due to their latest navigational skills, which enabled them to chart out towards the open seas without completely depending on visual cues from coastlines or landmasses. The evidence from archaeologists has also been declared in distant regions, which suggests the existence of Phoenician traders. Particularly, artefacts like pottery shards from the Atlantic coast of Spain and Portugal have been found. It is believed to be linked with the Phoenicians' trading activities during the 8th century BC era. Likewise, during this period, Tyre punched out the coins mined out by archaeological points around North Africa and Europe, which stipulated a worldwide commercial exchange network.

These suggest that during antiquity, the influence of Phoenicians was far-reaching. It developed the colonies all over the Mediterranean and discovered the new world in search of new opportunities for commerce and trade. Their founding spirit shaped much of our current knowledge regarding the practices of seafaring and navigation in this era.

The navigation and seafaring legacy of Phoenicians is present in ancient Greco-Roman texts, which demonstrates their journey towards distant lands. It only happened due to the advanced navigation skills which allowed them to take courses around the open seas without depending completely on the visual cues of coastlines and landmasses.

In ancient times, there was a desperate interest for the explorers to become part of advanced constructions for identity in Lebanon and Ireland. Particularly, the Lebanese government constructed the National Maritime Museum, which sought to reclaim their maritime heritage to preserve themselves in history. In addition to this era of ancient Irish exploration and trade routes, connections via past and current identities with archaeological evidence like Tyre minted the coins, which found that they can gain further insights all over North Africa and Europe to find how long-lasting the influence of Phoenicians was.

THE LEGACY OF PHOENICIAN NAVIGATION

Undoubtedly, the Phoenicians' expertise in shipbuilding and seamanship allowed them to create a roadmap for later civilisations. They played a pivotal role in helping the Greeks emerge from their Dark Ages and transition into the Iron Age. The historical transcripts of Greek and Roman civilisations offer evidence of using Phoenician seafaring techniques.

Also, the Phoenicians had a hand in shaping the foundation of Western civilisation. It is commonly observed that the roots of Western civilisation are intertwined with those of ancient Eastern civilisations like Egypt and Mesopotamia. According to the study, the Phoenicians undeniably left a lasting cultural influence on the Western world through their daring voyages. Furthermore, Irish scholars have claimed to have discovered trade routes across Europe by employing navigational techniques inspired by the Phoenicians.

Moreover, the navigation and seafaring legacy of the Phoenicians is present in ancient Greco-Roman texts, which demonstrates their journey towards distant lands. It only happened due to their advanced navigation skills, which allowed them to take courses around the open seas without depending completely on the visual cues of coastlines and landmasses.

In very ancient times, there was a desperate interest in the explorers to become part of advanced constructions for identity in Lebanon and Ireland. Particularly, the Lebanese government constructed the National Maritime Museum, which sought to reclaim its maritime heritage to preserve itself in history. In addition to this era of ancient Irish exploration and trade routes connections via past and current identities with archaeological evidence like Tyre minted the coins which founded that they can gain further insights all over North Africa and Europe to find how long-lasting the influence of Phoenicians was.

NAVIGATIONAL TOOLS AND TECHNIQUES

COASTAL NAVIGATION AND LANDMARKS

Undoubtedly, the Phoenicians left footsteps on numerous trade routes, thanks to their magnificent shipbuilding skills. These skills not only enabled them to embark on long-distance voyages but also empowered them to explore and discover many previously unknown territories. Their legacy as fearless explorers and masterful traders remains an awe-inspiring testament to their maritime achievements.

Besides celestial navigation, the Phoenicians ingeniously employed landmarks and coastal navigation techniques to venture far beyond the Mediterranean Sea. Throughout their extensive voyages, they strategically established numerous coastal landmarks, which also doubled as crucial trading outposts. This approach led to renowned trade hubs, with cities like Byblos, Tyre, and Sidon becoming synonymous with Phoenician navigation.

In essence, this unique navigational technique facilitated their maritime journeys and played a pivotal role in spreading their cultural influence and achieving remarkable trading success. Overall, it exemplifies their mastery in harnessing the environment to thrive in the world of ancient trade.

PHOENICIAN USE OF THE NORTH STAR FOR NAVIGATION

Most of the navigational techniques of the Phoenicians depended on the location of the stars. Wonderfully, the Phoenician civilisation discovered the use of the Polaris, a North star. In other words, they were behind using the celestial navigational techniques, in which ships can find direction in the sea.

Before using Polaris, ships tended to get close to the coastline to understand directions and avoid getting lost in the sea. For example, imagine you're in ancient Egypt and want to go to Anatolia. With this method, your ship would first have to sail east, following the coast of the Sinai Peninsula. Then, it would go north along the coast of Canaan. Finally, it would turn to the west and follow the coastline of Anatolia until it reaches its destination.

No wonder Phoenicians were deemed the first civilisation of the explorer. When ships didn't dare to go deep into the sea without losing sight of the coastline, there was no exploration and discovery of new trade routes and networks.

Once this technique was found, Phoenician navigators kept Polaris in their line of sight to understand the ship's direction and open more trade routes. This method also helped discover new places and save fuel to travel from one place to another by understanding celestial navigation instead of going close to the coastline.

It is safe to say that the Phoenicians' discovery of the celestial navigation technique was the foundation of the modern navigational techniques and tools, which are mentioned below.

ANCIENT NAVIGATION TOOLS

The mariner's compass was this era's oldest and earliest tool. It is a form of magnetic compass, a tool for navigation used by mariners. At the beginning of its invention, most of the mariners thought it was inaccurate and inconsistent because they were unaware of the concept of magnetic variation. Magnetic variation is the angle between the geographical north (a true north) and magnetic north. Its primary use was to point out the direction when the weather was clouded, due to which the sun became invisible to navigators or when the wind blew up.

In the 13th century, navigators realised maps would prove helpful for detailed voyage records. Due to this, the first nautical chart was created. However, these charts were not useful due to inaccuracy, but mariners kept them super-secret from others, just like a precious stone. This chart lacked the labelling of latitude or longitude but contained the compass rose, which indicated the direction of travel.

Cross-staff, Quadrant and astrolabe were early instruments to determine the latitude to assist the sailors. Astrolabe was first used by mariners at the end of the 15th century. It measured the altitude of the sun and star. In 1730, a tool known as the sextant was invented to measure an accurate angle between the sun, moon, stars, and horizon and measure the right latitude.

In the 16th century, an invention, the chip log, was used as a crude speedometer. Seaman used it to calculate the speed of a ship accurately by counting the number of knots present over regular intervals over a line. After that, the celestial navigation tool was invented. Celestial navigation is easily used completely to examine the latitude. Mariners could confirm latitude by determining the altitude of the North Star in the northern hemisphere above the horizon. The angle in degrees determines latitude.

Indeed, the Phoenicians were one of history's most successful ancient navigators. However, it is unfortunate that we don't have enough data to indicate that Phoenicians have used any of the above-mentioned navigational tools. Most of the Phoenician's navigation was done by observing the direction of the wind and the location of the sun and stars and using the primitive chart.

MODERN NAVIGATION TOOLS

A gyro compass was introduced to navigators in 1907. It was more useful than a magnetic compass because it is unaffected by the Earth's or ship's magnetic field and always pointed towards the north pole.

Radar, the greatest invention, was invented in 1935 to trace objects far away from the range of vision by projecting radio waves opposite the objects. This is still very useful to trace the ships and land when nothing is visible.

Loran, a long-range navigation system, developed between 1940 and 1943. It uses pulsed radio transmission waves to find out the exact location of other ships. It is highly accurate but has a very narrow range.

CELESTIAL NAVIGATION AND STAR CHARTS

Station Explorer for X-ray Timing and Navigation (XNAV) technology is the latest type of incarnation of celestial–based experiment for navigation. NASA has selected it for its next explorer mission. Its payload will utilise the world's most strange objects, pulsars, when it started the operation from its berth as a navigational beacon on the International Space Station in 2017. These objects are the subgroups of neutron stars, which rotate rapidly and emit powerful beams of light from the magnetic poles. To explain this method, the sextant will use detectors, 56 X-ray telescopes and other technologies to trace X-rays from strong beams of light to make estimations regarding the arrival of these pulses.

TRANSMISSION OF NAVIGATION KNOWLEDGE OF PHENOCIANS THROUGH GENERATIONS

Phoenicians were very dominant traders of the era or about two to three thousand years ago. They expanded from their homeland to construct new colonies and trading posts all over the Mediterranean, but suddenly, they vanished from history. We wanted to trace their male genetic traits in advanced populations. Well-detailed research was conducted in which new Y-chromosomal data was gathered from 1330 men. An analytical strategy was developed to find the linages, specifically associated with the Phoenicians, which were spread by geographically similar events but historically different. The results concluded that >6 per cent of the Phoenician signature to the modern Phoenician-influenced society.

It's intriguing to ponder how the Phoenicians passed down their shipbuilding and navigational knowledge from one generation to the next. Though, we don't find any data in this regard. While the exact method remains somewhat unclear, several possibilities come to mind. One potential approach could have been mentorship, where experienced sailors and shipbuilders guided and taught the younger generation.

Another common method, and perhaps the most likely, was learning from an early age. Children likely played a significant role in this process, assisting their parents during voyages and absorbing knowledge by closely observing and participating in maritime activities. This hands-on approach would have honed the Phoenicians' navigation and shipbuilding skills, starting from their earliest years.

PHOENICIAN NAVIGATORS IN HISTORY

This chapter is incomplete without the mention of some of the great Phoenician navigators in history. However, it is unfortunate that we don't have many historical traces to name the Phoenician navigators who pioneered trade through the sea, making it possible and easy. Nevertheless, there are some names we can extract from historical data, such as Solomon of the Ophir and King Hiram of Tyre.

Similarly, the names of Carthaginians Hanno and Himilcon are also mentioned in history. However, most of the data is found about the Periplus of Hanno. Hanno navigated the 5th century BC and conducted a journey towards the west coast of Africa for colonisation and exploration during the 5th century. He sailed out with 60 vessels which held 30,000 men and women, founded Kentitra (old Thymiaterion) and then constructed the temple at Cape Cantin. After that, he discovered five more within and across Morocco. The Essaouira was called the Carian Fortress on the coast of Morocco, where archaeologists found Punic settlers.

Furthermore, he founded Cerne as a trading post. Then, he reached further over the coast of Gambia and discovered as much as Cameroon. This complete journey had been written in Carthage at the temple of Bal. This complete story is now known as Periplus of Hannon.

Some Greek historians claim that the walls of the Melqart temple at Carthage once bore engraved transcripts about the voyages of Hanno. However, it's unfortunate that the Romans reportedly destroyed these inscriptions, leaving us with no clear testimony about their content.

As mentioned earlier, the navigator is known for his extensive journey along the African coast, where he discovered numerous coastal landmarks. The primary purpose of his expedition was reportedly to seek the riches and gold of Africa. The transcripts that were once associated with Hanno detail his journey from Carthage to the Pillars of Heracles.

However, advanced scholars have raised doubts about whether Hanno truly continued his journey along the Atlantic coast of Morocco. Some believe that the transcript mentions a very tall mountain called the "Chariot of the Gods," which they suspect might be the Mount Cameroon volcano (as previously mentioned). On the other hand, a third group of historians believes that he reached the Senegal River at the very least. There is no consensus on where his journey precisely concluded, but history has enshrined his name as a legendary Phoenician navigator.

SUMMARY

In general, shipbuilding, navigation, and seamanship were significant assets for Phoenician civilisation, enabling them to triumph in the battle for trading success and cultural influence. Navigators like Hanno left a legacy that later paved the way for the rise of Western civilisations. Consequently, their mastery of the sea facilitated easier sea trade and exploration of coastal regions, ultimately fostering diplomatic relations and leaving an enduring mark on history.

Chapter 2

BUILDING ROBUST TRADE NETWORKS

The Western Mediterranean coast was continuously settled from 11,000 BC and soon traded with areas such as Anatolia, the Levant, Egypt, and Greece. But trade wasn't always practised smoothly — in fact, there was a lot of political turbulence in ancient times that affected it. However, the Phoenicians arrived from the Levant and had a radically different approach.

They were the first civilisation to develop a maritime trading network and establish a vast empire across three continents. Their ships brought the finest of the empires' crafts, artisans, and goods – to their realms. But one unique thing they did was to live in harmony and make their network sustainable for the future. In this chapter, we will take you back in time to explore the alliances they built with other nations and learn from their invaluable experience.

PHOENICIAN MONOPOLIES

Phoenicians are known for their monopolies. It is because they were able to gain a monopoly over the trade of certain goods in the Mediterranean Sea. They earned this monopoly by having exclusive control over specific trading routes, making accessing them difficult for other traders. The Phoenicians also had an advantage over other traders because they had many ships that could be used for trade and military purposes. They had a monopoly on the production of purple dye, which they controlled by establishing trade networks in many regions around the Mediterranean. They also had a monopoly on transporting luxury goods like glass, ceramics, and metals.

The Phoenicians were able to establish these monopolies by exploiting their geographical location. They were situated at a crossroads of trade routes between Europe and Asia, which allowed them to control all aspects of the trade process and make significant profits.

The Phoenicians had a few key strategies to maintain their trade monopoly. First, they had to ensure their goods were higher quality than any other trader. It meant investing in better technology, better ships, and better sailors. They also had to ensure they didn't have competition from other traders by controlling the ports where they landed with force or persuasion.

PHOENICIAN TRADE NETWORKS IN ANTIQUITY

The Phoenician trade network was built on a foundation of mutual benefit. They traded with many different cultures, including those in Egypt and Rome, but they also traded with other

Phoenician cities. It meant that if a town was not doing well economically or politically, another would help by sending resources or money to support them until they could return.

They had good reason to be so successful—they had excellent ships. These ships could travel long distances, and they were very fast. The Phoenicians also had an excellent way of doing business: they would make agreements with other nations to have exclusive rights to trade with them for a set period. They would then travel back and forth between these nations and sell them things like cloth or glassware at high prices.

The Phoenicians were a trading people who lived in the Mediterranean from 1200 to 300 BCE. They are known for their seafaring and a love of luxury goods. The Phoenicians were great innovators in sailing technology and shipbuilding, and they developed several tools for navigation.

Phoenician trade routes were extensive. They would sail from their home city of Tyre (modern-day Lebanon) to Carthage (in modern Tunisia) via Cyprus and Crete, then continue to Rhodes and Mycenae. From there, they sailed westward to Sardinia, Spain, and Sicily before heading north towards Italy or eastward toward Greece.

The most valuable commodities that the Phoenicians traded were metals such as copper, tin, lead, and silver; timber products such as cedar wood; dyes made from plants like madder root; ivory tusks; glass beads; aromatic oils like myrrh; perfume oils like oleander flower oil; wine made with grapes grown on Cyprus; iron weapons in addition to bronze ones; pottery items such as bowls made from clay mixed with water from a red clay deposit called "red earth" found near Tyre.

USING A REPRESENTATIVE

The Phoenicians had a reputation for being master traders. But what made them so good at it?

One of their most essential advantages was their use of an expert. This person would travel to foreign lands and build relationships with the local merchants and traders, who were then able to provide information about the quality and price of goods in that area. The expert representative would then return to Tyre or Sidon (the two main Phoenician ports) and report. Merchants in Tyre or Sidon would then use this information to decide which goods were worth trading for or whether they should continue dealing with one merchant or trader from a specific port. This system allowed merchants from Tyre or Sidon to make informed decisions about how much money they were willing to spend on certain goods and how much profit they could expect when selling those goods after importing them back into their home city's marketplace.

PHOENICIAN EXPANSION IN ANCIENT GREECE

Their influence can be seen in the architecture of many ancient cities, including Carthage and Cádiz, as well as their cultural influence on the Greeks. Their impact on Greek culture is evident in many aspects of their culture, including architecture and art forms such as pottery and jewellery. They also influenced language by introducing new words into Greek that were derived from their language.

The Phoenicians were a Semitic people who were among the first to engage in trade across the Mediterranean Sea. Most of their trade was centred around the city-state of Tyre. The Phoenicians also brought many innovations to the area, including the alphabet and writing materials like papyrus. They established several colonies in mainland Greece and Sicily, including Carthage (named after their homeland) and Utica. These colonies often served as trading posts where they could buy raw materials like silver, tin, wool, and grain from the local population and then sell them back to their homeland or other locations along the coast.

CARTHAGE CREATED A STRONG FOUNDATION
Carthage was the centre of trade in the Western Mediterranean from 800 BC to 146 BC. Phoenicians founded the city, and it became a major port for their trading ships.

The Carthaginians had a strong foundation in trade that would lead them to dominate trade routes for centuries. They were able to establish a strong mercantile community that was able to expand throughout the Mediterranean Sea and beyond.

The Carthaginians established themselves as a powerful trading empire. They used their wealth to build an impressive navy and waged war against their neighbours to control these trade routes.

THE PHOENICIANS OF CARTHAGE BUILT UP THE COASTAL TRADE ROUTES

They significantly impacted the entire region's development, including Greece and Rome.

The Phoenicians were a people who lived in what is now Lebanon and Syria. They developed a very advanced civilisation that was based on trade and commerce. They created cities along the eastern coast of the Mediterranean Sea, where they could establish trading posts with other countries. In addition to trading with other countries, they also traded within their territory. The Phoenicians were known for their skills as sailors and navigators. They were able to navigate large ships as far as Britain and Ireland.

The Phoenicians were famous for their ability to build strong trade networks throughout Europe and Africa. They established colonies throughout these areas so that they could access raw materials from these areas without having to travel through them themselves (which would have been difficult).

THE PHOENICIAN CITY-STATES MERGED AS THE PUNIC EMPIRE FOR MORE CONTROL OF THE MEDITERRANEAN
The Phoenician city-states merged as the Punic Empire reached out for more control of the Mediterranean. The empire was based in Carthage, which was in what is now Tunisia. The

Phoenician language became extinct around this time, but their culture influenced many other cultures in the Mediterranean region.

As trade increased across the Mediterranean Sea, Punic traders established colonies throughout Western Europe and North Africa. The Punic Empire eventually rose to power after defeating Carthage's ancient rival in Spain during the Third Punic War (149-146 BC). By this time, Carthage had grown into a significant power with territory from Spain into modern-day Tunisia. This conflict resulted in Rome taking control over Carthage after defeating it during its war against Hannibal Barca.

THE ACCOMPLISHMENTS OF THE PHOENICIANS ARE STILL EVIDENT TODAY

The achievements of this ancient civilisation are so remarkable that they continue to impact the world in ways that many people don't realise. For example, their trade networks were so robust that they helped spread knowledge and culture across ancient civilisations and continents. The Phoenicians also helped develop the alphabet, which many other civilisations would later use throughout history.

Even today, we use words derived from the Phoenician language every day: cinnamon, carnelian, myrrh, and papyrus all come from this ancient culture. While most people know about their contributions to navigation via their discovery of the magnetic compass and their development of advanced sailing techniques (such as square-rigged ships), fewer people know about how these discoveries affected daily life for citizens in ancient Greece and Rome—and even later civilisations such as Russia or China!

Even though these accomplishments happened thousands of years ago, it's clear that today's world would look very different without them!

LOSING CONTROL TO THEIR TRADE NETWORKS WAS A REAL THREAT

The Phoenicians had to be innovative and proactive to maintain their trading power. They had built their entire economy around trade, so losing that would have been disastrous. Luckily, they could expand their network by connecting with other cultures and developing new technology.

Their cities were centres of innovation, as they made advances in agriculture and metallurgy. They had to be able to adapt when other civilisations came into power or interfered with their trading routes. They created new ideas around farming and metalworking. It allowed them to produce higher-quality goods than before. One way they were able to do this is through innovation.

BUSINESSES SHOULD LEARN FROM PHOENICIAN STRATEGIES

The Phoenicians were an ancient civilisation that lived in the Mediterranean and North Africa. They were known for their trade networks, spreading their influence throughout the region.

They have much to teach us about business strategy and management. Let's look at some of their strategies:

They understood that salesmanship and reliability of service were critical. They ensured they delivered what they promised, even if it meant going out of their way or making sacrifices. It was key to maintaining trust with their customers and ensuring repeat business.

They valued efficiency over all else—even at the expense of quality! For example, they would use whatever materials were available to them without worrying about whether it was the "best" material available; instead, they focused on using what they had available efficiently and effectively to get the job done as quickly as possible (and thus save money).

3. They believed in keeping things simple: Their ships had few parts and no external decorations; they used simple designs for houses; they did not strive for grandeur in any way (but kept things simple). It helped them save money while making it easier for new workers unfamiliar with how things worked.

HOW PHOENICIANS COMMUNICATED

Their language was one of their most enduring legacies. The Phoenician alphabet was used to write their language and other languages. It is believed that the Greeks borrowed much from the Phoenicians when they created their alphabet, which is still in use today.

To communicate with each other and with others around the Mediterranean Sea, they had to learn how to use this new alphabet with ease.

The most common form of communication among the Phoenicians was through flags. They raised flags to show that something important was on board or someone needed assistance. They used flags to communicate with other ships in case of an emergency at sea, or someone needed help.

HOW PHOENICIANS OUTMATCHED COMPETITION

The Phoenician people were able to produce various goods in their homeland, and they exported these goods throughout their empire. They traded with other cultures across Europe, Asia, Africa, and North America by bartering with items like silver jewellery, pottery, and glassware."

The Phoenicians were responsible for introducing many innovations into commerce, such as gold coins for international trade, standardised weights and measures, bulk cargo carriers, double-hulled ships with sails, cedar wood from Lebanon, glassmaking techniques, purple dye from murex shells, papyrus paper from Egypt - all of which contributed to their success in trade.

HOW PHOENICIANS FORMED PARTNERSHIPS

Phoenicians were known for their innovative business practices. They worked in partnerships, which allowed them to share the risk of starting a new venture or expanding an existing one. The partnership would also allow them access to capital to create or expand their business.

Partnerships were also helpful because they allowed several people with different skills and areas of expertise to work together on a project. It meant that the group would get more done in less time and that each person could focus on what they were best at—such as managing finances or building boats—and not worry about things they were not as skilled at doing.

HOW PHOENICIANS SAILED THE WAVES TO SUCCESS

The Phoenicians were master sailors who built an empire spanning the Mediterranean Sea, and they did it all without a map. They navigated by stars, sun, and moon and had a triangulation system to help them chart their course. When the Greeks stole their knowledge of navigation and astronomy (which they taught them), it was called "triangulation."

What does this have to do with businesses? Well, it shows us that sometimes we don't need a map to succeed—we must be willing to take risks and keep going until we get there!

SUMMARY

It is, thus, evident that these Phoenician traders and businesses were able to build their trade networks robustly. They succeeded because they stuck to a simple strategy based on deep research and flexible adaptation to vastly different conditions. What can we learn from the success of these far-reaching early merchant networks?

Traders, even today, could benefit from expanding into larger markets by forging sites for industry plans and new productive capacity infrastructure. With a closer look at the Phoenician trade model, we can see they were able to do this over 2,000 years ago. Their methodologies still have a lot to teach modern traders and businesses about maintaining robust networks.

What is clear from this comparison is that there are no secrets to running a successful trading business and that careful, hard work always pays off in the end. Modern businesses can leverage the experience of ancient business people by studying how they did business and how they kept strong trade networks alive for centuries. Each one of these businesses was the result of a small start-up. There is nothing that says your small business must be any different.

Anyone can have a successful commerce experience by following Phoenician concepts of business.

Chapter 3

CULTURAL ADAPTABILITY AND MARKET EXPANSION

The previous chapter discussed how the Phoenicians used their experience to achieve success in trade and commerce. However, it allowed them to expand their fleet even more. Yet, their great knowledge of sea routes was helpful for their expansion policies. How long had they been trading with different cultures and civilisations? However, it is a fact that they were one of the earliest nations to have traded with Greece, Turkey, Egypt, Syria, and other civilisations that were popular in West Asia during their time. With a comprehensive insight into the main Phoenician cities, we continue to analyse different aspects of their cultural adaptability and market development.

PHOENICIANS ARE DESCENDENT OF THE CANAANITES

The Phoenicians were also outstanding builders and great seafarers and traders. They were responsible for many architectural achievements, such as cathedrals and temples throughout Europe and Asia Minor during the first millennium BC--including famous sites like the Acropolis in Athens.

Their ships could carry large cargoes, and they developed many innovations that made sailing safer, such as sails that could be adjusted easily to the wind direction.

The Phoenicians also used a form of alphabet called the Proto-Canaanite alphabet, written right to left on clay tablets. This alphabet was later adapted for use by Hebrews and Greeks when they adopted writing systems from them.

The Phoenicians were also known for their ability to adapt to different environments and cultures. It enabled them to establish trade relations with many other regional civilisations. The Phoenicians are credited with introducing Greek culture to northern Africa. The Phoenicians also expanded their trading empire into Spain, Sicily, and Sardinia.

The success of these seafaring traders was partly due to their ability to adapt culturally—they were not just traders but also explorers who explored new territories and introduced new ideas from other cultures into their society.

The Phoenicians used their knowledge of geography and navigation to establish colonies throughout the Mediterranean region. Each colony was run by a local ruler who reported to someone more powerful back home in Phoenicia. The Phoenicians traded with many cultures, including the Greeks, Assyrians, Egyptians, and Persians. They were also skilled merchants who traded with other nations outside of those mentioned above; however, they tended to favour trade with groups that had similar cultural values or religious beliefs as themselves to feel comfortable doing business in foreign lands where they might not speak each other's languages or understand their cultures fully yet still maintain some sense of familiarity between them all regardless (e.g., both parties worshipped Baal).

The Phoenicians were known for their technological innovations and ability to readily adapt when faced with new challenges or circumstances at home and abroad. This allowed them to thrive when others struggled due to lack thereof.

Their ability to adapt was also reflected in their business practices. The Greeks referred to them as "Punians," which means "people who live on islands" or "islanders." The Romans called them "Phoenices," which means "people who live in purple." This nickname was given because they imported fabrics from dyes extracted from sea snails found near Sardinia—a practice that monopolised this resource and made them quite wealthy.

There is no dispute that the Phoenicians were influential in developing some of the world's first modern nations and even some of the world's first cities.

PHOENICIANS ACCEPTED DIFFERENCES IN CULTURE ACROSS THEIR TRADES

Phoenician traders were able to adapt to different cultural norms across their trades. It is because they were not ethnocentric, meaning they didn't believe in the superiority of their own culture. They saw themselves as a business and adapted to the customs wherever they went.

The Phoenicians were also unique because they accepted cultural differences across their trades. It was an integral part of what made them such successful merchants: when you're trying to deal with people from other cultures, it helps to accept their differences and similarities!

Additionally, while some people may be surprised by this acceptance, it makes sense when we consider that they lived in an area constantly changing hands between different groups.

Phoenician traders were known to be highly adaptable and accepted differences in culture across their trades. They did not force their beliefs or traditions on the people they traded with. They learned from each other and often adapted their products to fit customers' tastes.

These traders were also tolerant of religious and political differences. Their trade partners had different gods and beliefs, and the Phoenicians did not try to force them to change their practices or beliefs. The Phoenicians also allowed other people to rule over them without conflict. Even though foreign kings ruled them, they did not fight against them.

They expanded their trade routes across the Mediterranean and as far as Britain. Their culture was diverse and tolerant of other cultures, which made it easier for them to interact with people

21

from other regions. The Phoenicians also adapted their trade routes to meet the needs of many different cultures, which helped them spread their influence across a wide area.

INDICATIONS OF TOLERANCE: PHOENICIANS' OPENNESS TO OTHER CULTURES

The Phoenician culture was a highly adaptable one, which is why it was able to spread across the Mediterranean for centuries. It can be seen in their material culture, which is full of influences from other cultures.

The Phoenicians were tolerant of outside influence and took on many aspects of the cultures they traded with. Artefacts recovered from Phoenician sites show that they wore Greek-style jewellery and Egyptian-style clothing and even had a taste for Persian textiles. Paintings on tomb walls also demonstrate this openness: some depict scenes from Greek mythological stories, while others depict Egyptian deities like Isis or Osiris.

This openness allowed the Phoenicians to spread across the Mediterranean region, as they could integrate into each new culture without resistance from those already living there.

It suggests that the Phoenicians were not just accepting of difference but actively sought it out; they did not try to impose their cultural values on other cultures through colonisation, which would be an attitude characteristic of a closed-minded culture.

SKILFUL NAVIGATION OF FOREIGN MARKETS LED TO WEALTH, INFLUENCE, AND POWER

The Phoenicians' adaptation was not only cultural; it was also geographic. The ports where the Phoenicians traded were often located far from home, so they had to adapt their practices and methods of transporting goods from one shoreline to another.

They were skilled navigators, and their ability to navigate foreign markets led to wealth, influence, and power beyond what first seemed possible. Their skill at navigating the world was so great that they became known as the great explorers of their time. An encounter with the people of Cyprus also inspired outstanding achievement in Tyre - they were determined not to be left behind if their rivals could make successful trade contacts.

PHOENICIAN SHIPPING AND TRADING FAR EXCEEDED THEIR COMPETITORS

The Phoenicians had a thriving culture that included art, architecture, science, mathematics, astronomy and religion. They were also skilled at metalworking and glass blowing, but their navigational skills set them apart from other civilisations of their day.

The name of Phoenicians comes from the Greek word for "purple" because they were known to dye fabric with a purple colour from murex snails. The Phoenicians were also known for their glasswork and metalwork skills and their knowledge of alchemy and medicine.

The Phoenicians established colonies throughout the Mediterranean Sea, including Carthage (now Tunisia) and Cadiz (Spain). They also traded extensively with Egypt, where they traded ivory, spices, glassware, perfumes, wine, pottery, and other goods from their homeland. In fact, this trade helped establish Egypt as one of the most powerful nations in the region at that time.

The Phoenician ships were highly advanced compared to other vessels being used at that time by other nations such as Greece or Rome due partly to their use of oars rather than sails, which allowed them to navigate into shallow waters where other ships could not go without getting stuck on rocks or sandbars!

They made beautiful glass beads from melted sand, which could be used as currency during trade negotiations because they were considered precious metals due to their rarity (and thus value) at that period.

When it comes to business, Phoenicia was and still is a model of success. With a successful trading empire reaching various parts of the Mediterranean world, the Phoenicians established an economic empire that showed traders everywhere that one doesn't need to be big or have centuries of history to achieve great things in business.

ADAPTABILITY: THE PHOENICIAN KEY TO TRADE EXPANSION

The Phoenicians could adapt to their environment and use it to their advantage. They were not afraid to sail into unknown waters and could use tools such as the astrolabe to navigate across oceans. The Greeks would later copy this tool from them.

They would travel far and wide to find new resources and connect with other civilisations. They could adapt to different environments and cultures, which allowed them to expand their trading empire greatly.

It meant they could easily adapt to new climates and weather conditions, which helped them expand their global reach. The Phoenician empire grew rapidly due to their ability to adapt easily, making it possible for them to travel further than anyone else then!

The Phoenician's adaptability made them one of the most successful trading civilisations in history. They also deeply understood astronomy and mathematics, which helped them understand the movement of stars and planets. It allowed them to navigate their ships safely through dangerous waters without relying on landmarks or other visual cues like different cultures did at the time.

As trading becomes increasingly complicated, adaptable traders will succeed. Today's fast-paced, high-stakes trading environment is too complex for rigid systems to contain. The best traders are willing and able to tweak their strategies on the fly based on market fluctuations, personal experience, and intuition. It's the trait that separates winners from losers and will serve them well in the future.

DIASPORA CULTURE

The Phoenician diaspora culture is characterised by its ability to adapt to new environments while maintaining its unique cultural identity. One example of this can be seen in how many Phoenician people settled in North Africa during their travels through the Mediterranean region. They brought their culture with them when they settled in North Africa but were able to adapt it to fit into their new environment. For example, some scholars argue that the Phoenician alphabet helped inspire similar alphabets used by other civilisations throughout history, such as Greek or Hebrew letters used today (Nagel).

Another way we see this cultural adaptability is expressed through religion; many early Christians considered themselves part of a Jewish-Christian tradition because they saw themselves from origin.

The Phoenician diaspora began when these seafaring people began migrating around the Mediterranean region in search of new trade opportunities. As they established new colonies, they brought their culture along with them so that each territory would be familiar with its home culture even though it was now thousands of miles away from its original location in present-day Lebanon or Syria (or both).

You must respect your trade if you want to succeed in the markets. No one knows that better than the Phoenicians, and they could teach us a thing or two about how to engage with the market with respect and love for your craft.

MOTHER HUBS

The Phoenicians had many hubs around the Mediterranean. The main hub was Tyre, where most of their trade happened. The Phoenicians also had other smaller hubs in places like Cyprus, Carthage, and Sicily.

The Phoenicians highly valued their cultural adaptability, so they did not have one set of laws or one way of doing things. Instead, they allowed each city/state to have its laws and customs regarding everything from religion to trade practices. It made it easier for them to expand into different cultures because they did not have to change their culture when they moved to another place.

They also valued market expansion, so they always looked for new ways to make money by trading with other civilisations around the Mediterranean Sea.

THE IONIAN EXCHANGE

The Phoenicians were a society of traders and explorers. From the earliest days of their civilisation, they had been a part of the Ionian Exchange, a trade route that connected East and

West. They even founded colonies in other parts of the Mediterranean, including Carthage (in modern-day Tunisia), considered one of their most successful trading settlements.

However, as time passed, this exchange became increasingly important to them. It gave them access to goods from all over the world, including spices from India and China, foods like almonds and pistachios, and even materials like gold and silver. It allowed them to expand their empire even further across the Mediterranean Sea.

Their expansion continued until it peaked during King Solomon's reign. He built an impressive temple in Jerusalem called Solomon's Temple. Today, it is still considered one of history's most magnificent structures, along with several others throughout his kingdom (including one in Lebanon). However, these temples were destroyed during an invasion by Assyrians under King Sennacherib.

The ancient Phoenicians were experts in the trading industry. This is obvious given the size and scope of Phoenician trade networks that spanned the entire Mediterranean Sea during their era. Even for traders today, with our technological innovations and advancements, many of us still follow in their footsteps through a similar trading style.

SUMMARY

Through the study of ancient Phoenician trade routes and the analysis of artefacts found across the Mediterranean and Middle Eastern regions, we can determine that the Ancient Phoenicians were, at one point, more influential traders than even the Greeks or Romans. Their origin in modern-day Lebanon is still hotly contested. However, their extensive trade network filled with colonies worldwide made them a dominant power in a period where many were vying for control. Their trading of food, wine, metals, statues, and art helped to spread their culture far beyond its original location.

In conclusion, the Phoenicians originated along the Mediterranean Sea, settled in parts of Lebanon, and expanded to neighbouring areas. The Phoenicians were most likely excellent navigators and merchants, as they could find their way across the Mediterranean Sea and expand into many ports. They were innovative people who developed many useful tools still being used today. For several reasons, Phoenicians remain the most versatile and adaptive culture to be redacted. The characteristics of its followers are expressed and preserved in a visual language known as negative space. This is a convenient medium for any culture that has matured and evolved into the future realm of fluidity.

Understanding cultural adaptability when expanding production to different markets is critical to success. By outfitting Phoenicians with transducers allowed them to become more adaptable under any circumstances and saved money as they were working only fifteen minutes a week on "talking slowly."

Chapter 4

ORGANIZATIONAL LOGISTICS AND EFFICIENCY

The Phoenicians were well known for their organisational logistics and efficiency in the maritime trade. Their civilisation was comprised of numerous independent states. Every state has its trade options. It provides them an opportunity for decentralised operations and high efficiency in regional trade.

The modern shipping companies of today's world can easily adopt a decentralised approach. It can be done by incorporating multiple hubs and ports to streamline operations. Through this, you can easily get access to specific markets efficiently.

Phoenicians were also very skilled shipbuilders. They have crafted many vessels, including Trireme and Bireme. All the ships that they designed were outstanding in speed and operation. It makes them ideal for exploration as well as for trade operations. By utilising these outstanding and advanced ship designs, modern companies can easily enhance their shipping competitiveness. It can be done in terms of speed, cargo capacity, and fuel efficiency.

The Phoenicians have also established a big network of trade routes. They have made colonies in the Mediterranean region. Through this, they were able to access distant places very easily. All these routes help them access a wide range of markets and resources. This is also a lesson for modern shipping companies that they can easily access diverse markets by developing global trade routes. It can also optimise cargo transportation if it strategically locates its trading hubs.

The Phoenicians also had efficient storage and loading processes on the ports that they developed. They facilitate rapid goods transfer. This all shows their high logistic efficiency. So, by handling the cargo processes very efficiently and all the storage operations, today's modern world companies can easily minimise delays. They can also optimise the logistic efficiency of modern shipping companies.

The Phoenicians were known for innovating different technologies and tools for optimising logistics and trade. They employed many new technology techniques to enhance maritime and Logistics operations. Phoenicians created advanced ship designs, celestial navigation, landmarks, rudimentary maps, efficient loading and unloading operations, resource extraction, and extensive trade routes. They have also used relay systems and have adapted all the operations for geo-political civilisation. Their construction technique and designs were adapted to the required conditions and needs.

PHOENICIAN PORT MANAGEMENT AND LOGISTICAL INNOVATIONS

The Phoenicians have made a huge name in efficient port management. They have also excelled in the skills of logistical innovations. They play a very important role in the maritime trade. Following are some of the strategies for port management and logistical innovations that the Phoenicians adopted in the ancient world.

STRATEGIC LOCATION:

The Phoenicians have always carefully selected the locations of ports. The locations have been favourable according to the Geographic area. It has always favoured geographical features like deep water or natural harbours. This has allowed them to facilitate smooth unloading operations. This is one of the best strategies adopted by the Phoenicians in ancient times throughout the Mediterranean region to enhance trade.

AMAZING INFRASTRUCTURE:

The Phoenicians constructed amazing breakwaters and pairs by using timber and stone. These are the durable materials used in constructing the infrastructure of the ports. This infrastructure provided a big space for accommodation for many vessels. It also improves the efficiency of handling goods and passengers at the ports.

SKILLED HARBOUR MAN:

The Phoenicians have employed experienced staff at the ports and harbours. This staff possesses amazing skills and extensive knowledge of the weather and water patterns. They had great expertise in ensuring the ship's optimal arrival and departure. They also avoid any delay in loading and unloading operations.

SECURITY MEASURES:

To ensure the safety of ports from any unauthorised entry or piracy, the permissions have built outstanding security measures. They have built defensive walls and gates on the ports. All these measures were taken to ensure the safety of cargo personnel and the ships. These safety measures highlight the Phoenicians' affected port management and logistic innovations.

STREAMLINING OPERATIONS FOR CONTEMPORARY SHIPPING COMPANIES

Modern ship companies can learn numerous lessons from ancient civilisations. The efficiency of Phoenicians in logistics offers valuable lessons. All these lessons apply to the modern logistics and supply chain management. The following are some of the lessons explained in detail that modern companies must learn:

Modern logistic operations must be prioritised in the structure development. This is done to streamline smooth operations. It will help you in providing more success and profit in return.

They traded numerous goods, which helped them become an independent civilisation. They don't depend on only a single resource but trade for various goods. So, modern supply chain management companies must diversify the product offerings of their companies. This will reduce the risk that is associated with single resources and products.

The skilled labour force is also a very integral strategy that modern companies should adopt. The Phoenician's logistics comprised skilled labour driving mass success and wealth. So, training and employing professionals and experienced personnel in the logistics and supply chain management department will make it easy for the companies to progress. It is a key factor in introducing efficient operations throughout the company in logistics.

Modern logistics should also focus on effective communication factors. This will ensure that the stakeholders are always informed about everything. It will create a big network between distant regions as well. So, incorporating amazing communication networks and relay systems will facilitate a good flow of logistics operations. The Phoenicians did it in the past, which allowed them to succeed in the Mediterranean region.

Security measures should also be taken to protect the cargo in the logistics company's ports. Modern logistics should also focus on cargo security to prevent any damage.

In the past, the Phoenicians depended on the overland relay systems. These relay systems were also used to provide great information in distant regions. So, like the Phoenicians, modern logistics can also get a big lesson from them. They can also benefit from the robust tracking and data-sharing systems.

Modern logistics companies should also focus on sustainability. They should align with the growing importance of eco-friendly purchases by focusing on sustainability and environmental impact so they can grow well. So, by incorporating all these lessons from the Phoenicians, efficiency in the logistics. In the modern world, supply chain companies can benefit easily. Different principles, including adaptability, scaled labour, and diversification, can help modern companies grow in global trade. It will allow their business to optimise all the trade and logistic operations and help them compete.

TOOLS AND TECHNOLOGY FOR OPTIMISING LOGISTICS

The Phoenicians were known for creating numerous tools and technology to facilitate trade. They have made many records in the trade industry based on archaeological findings and historical research. Following are some of the tools and technology developed by the Phoenicians.

The cargo manifest and records were crucial for tracking the goods the traders transported in the Mediterranean region. They maintain records with the help of the alphabet that they had developed in ancient times. It was used for written documentation.

They have also devised a tool known as Tally sticks. These Tally sticks were used to record goods across different cultures. The Phoenicians used these tally sticks to keep track of quantities, transactions, and all other relevant data related to trade activities and those goods.

Along with the written records, they developed mnemonic techniques as well. They have played a very important role in transmitting trade-related information through communication. It helps them in creating a very strong network and extensive navigational skills. It helps them know about the cargo destination and the trade route.

Nowadays, different modern logistical tools are used to increase Logistics science. They have taken many lessons from the ancient civilisation. These logistical tools include GPS tracking, Data Analytics, and inventory management. These are essential tools that have revolutionised the businesses of modern companies.

- GPS tracking helps in real-time monitoring of your goods and shipments. It helps you track your different assets with the help of GPS tracking or GPS technology. The companies can easily determine the location of the vehicles or goods. It is also useful for ensuring the safety and timely delivery. It helps in optimising the logistical operations and monitoring your businesses.

- Secondly, inventory management software helps provide a centralised inventory management system. It also allows you to have an efficient monitoring of stock levels. You will get a very streamlined order processing with the help of inventory management software. This software helps you in mitigating the risk of stock out or understocking.

- Data Analytics is also a powerful tool for modern businesses that helps them get valuable insights into their data. It will help you in enhancing the smoothness of logical activities. With the help of data analytics, different modern organisations can easily analyse past performance and current market trends. It also helps in understanding customer behaviour and supports the planning for the future growth of the business.

All these modern logistical tools provide efficiency, cost production, and increase customer satisfaction. By using GPS tracking, Data Analytics, and inventory management software, modern businesses can easily optimise the supply chain and make correct decisions that will impact their business positively.

LOGISTICAL ORGANISATION

The Phoenician's logistical system involved various specialised ships to send different goods. It was used for efficient transportation of goods to different places. All these shapes played a very important role in maritime trade and in enhancing logistics operations. The ships were used to make the transportation of specific goods.

29

The Phoenicians used merchant vessels. They were very versatile and transported a huge variety of goods. They were used for transporting bulk products. The products mainly include metals, textiles, and other big items. Warships were also present in the ancient civilisation used by the Phoenicians in logistical operations. They were very helpful in protecting the trade operations. The warships used were fast and best for warfare.

There were Tyrian Purple ships as well. These ships were specialised and developed only for collecting the snails through which the Purple dye was obtained. The ships were only specialised for producing and transferring the Tyrian Purple dye to different areas. Bulk cargo ships were also present. These ships transferred different goods, including building materials and green crops. The Phoenicians used these bulk cargo ships to store many products. These cargo ships were used to transfer bulk cargo efficiently.

CARGO SPECIALIZATION AND TIMELY DELIVERY:

Cargo specialisation plays a very important role in the field of logistics. It helps provide you with efficient transportation. There will be completely secure transportation of your goods. The entire handling process will be safe and according to your storage requirements. One of the primary importance of cargo specialisation is its enhanced deficiency. If you focus mainly on cargo types, you can easily develop expertise in goods handling. As a result, it leads to high accuracy, improved speed, and reliability in transporting various goods. This will help you quickly deliver your goods with reduced risk of goods with the help of cargo specialisation. You can receive a good customer feedback. It will help you grow your business and have a competitive edge in the logistics market. It helps in a helping Logistics providers gain long-term partnerships. It also helps in building a strong relationship in the trade industry. It is one of the main things in logistical operations with increased efficiency, safety, and customer satisfaction. So, businesses can easily optimise their operations with the help of cargo specialisation techniques.

Today, modern businesses can easily apply the cargo specialisation strategy to enhance logistic operations.

A company that sells perishable goods like vegetables, medicine, or fruits can easily purchase refrigerated foods. They will help in providing a fresh delivery of your goods. It will develop handling expertise in considering delicate items. So, by implementing quality control measures, you can easily ensure the freshness and quality of the perishable goods. It will prevent them from spoilage.

If you are running a company in which you must transfer hazardous materials, then it must require expertise and safety regulations. As such, companies sending hazardous substances cargo must train their employees in proper handling techniques. This will help them ensure the safety and compliance of their goods. It will also increase the timely delivery and guarantee the security of your chemicals or other hazardous substances.

Companies focusing on transporting oversize or heavyweight cargo can use trains and trailers. These items may include construction equipment or any other machinery equipment. It will help you in making the infrastructure development easy and reliable. If you specialise in material handling, you can also provide efficient services to different industries.

Therefore, modern companies can easily develop expertise by focusing on cargo specialisation. They can invest in specialised resources and then provide their services that are available with security and reliability. It will also ensure customer satisfaction and market competitiveness.

SUMMARY

The Phoenician's port management and logistic innovation have made many advancements and successes in the ancient world. They had a great mastery of the maritime trade. Many port facilities were available because of the Phoenicians across the Mediterranean region. Their innovations help in facilitating trade. All these tools and techniques they devised play a vital role in economic prosperity. The Phoenicians contributed a lot to enhancing the logistic operations and trade on pints.

Today, modern businesses should also embrace this technology and strategies to get efficient organisational logistics. This will help them elevate the customer experience and the company's operations. It will also grow the operational efficiency and bring advancement in their field. They can easily get more opportunities, and the risk will be eliminated from their business.

Chapter 5

MARKET ADAPTION AND INNOVATION

The Phoenicians have made many outstanding contributions to the trade innovation in their era. They had great expertise in commerce and maritime exploration, which helped them establish the trade routes. They were the first people to transform the commerce industry radically. These people made many innovations and spread many new technologies in the Mediterranean region. Examples of their innovations include introducing oil production in Italy and Spain, horse riding in North Africa and Egypt, and introducing several new products. All these innovations help in increasing the economic growth in their region. They also introduced many crops and other farming techniques. The Phoenicians maintain their competitiveness in the global market by implementing different strategies.

They recognise the importance of diverse products. The Phoenicians created a variety of goods with the help of specialised industries that they developed in their areas. A huge variety of goods were introduced in different markets. They also recognise the importance of diplomatic relations. In an attempt to build skilful negotiation and diplomatic relations, they built strong relations with the neighbouring civilisations and states.

It helped them create a very favourable trade bond, and they also got great access to the market of different states. This also helps them resolve conflicts and gives them a great advantage in the product market. They have also cultivated many crops. These plants may include grapes, wheat, olives, barley, and wine. They produced all these products to provide comfort and benefit to the people of the Mediterranean region. Their irrigation system was also established, and growth increased over time.

PHOENICIAN CONTRIBUTIONS TO TRADE INNOVATION

There are different ways in which Phoenicians innovated much in the trade sector. They created many new technologies and innovative new products that were helpful for the people of that era. Those products are also used nowadays and are very beneficial to humanity.

One of the best techniques that they developed was in the field of agriculture. They developed a great irrigation system. This irrigation system was also used to produce crops in the dry seasons. In the dry Seasons, it was done by changing the way of water from the river to the water canals. From the water canals, the water was passed to the crop fields where they were planted. They also discovered a method of crop rotation. It helps increase and maintain soil fertility. Many plants were under their supervision. They include grapes, Olive, Barley, and wheat.

Metalworking is also a very innovative technique that they discovered. They produced bronze weapons and sculptures with elephant tusks. Many different metals like bronze, gold, and silver were produced, which increased the economy of the Phoenicians.

They also developed a weight measurement system. This helps the merchants in weighing the items accurately. It mainly helps them in trading. So, it was a great innovation to increase trade and commerce in their area.

The Phoenicians have also introduced the first alphabets. These alphabets were the base for the invention of many alphabets. They include Greek, Latin and English alphabets. It was a great creation by them, which helped them communicate more effectively. As a result, it benefited them in trade and commerce purposes. It facilitates them in record keeping and trade documentation.

They also develop techniques for shipbuilding. The Phoenicians constructed ships that travelled from one place to another with large amounts of goods. They help in providing a great economy.

Wine production was also an essential component of their economy at that time. It was produced from grapes. The wine was also a highly traded good of the Phoenicians.

All these innovative techniques help them in producing a huge number of goods for export. As a result, it enhances their wealth. Also, their power and name were increased throughout the Mediterranean region. All these innovations had a great impact on the economy as well as on their culture. These things were necessary for their heritage and made them succeed worldwide. The Phoenicians introduced many new technologies that are alive today as well.

STRATEGIES FOR STAYING COMPETITIVE

The Phoenicians have employed numerous strategies for staying competitive in the rising market.

SEAFARING:

They had great expertise in seafaring. They were well-known shipbuilders as well as sailors. The Phoenicians built advanced ships that took cargo from one place to another. It helped them explore new markets and establish new trade routes very easily. Seafaring was among the best strategies for increasing their position and worth in the trade sector.

GEOGRAPHICAL REGION:

They had a great advantage of their Geographic region. The strategic location of the Phoenicians in the Mediterranean helped them connect numerous civilisations. They act as an intermediate for trade between different states. They help in controlling many key points of different states in the field of commerce.

CULTURAL ADAPTATION:

Phoenicians also need high strategies for cultural adaptability. They adapted to different languages and customs of different regions and religions. It helps them in creating a good relationship with other states. This also helped them facilitate trade in the Mediterranean region with high accuracy.

TRADING OF RESOURCES:

They started trading different resources, which helped them grow their economy. There were various commodities, including dye, metals, and wood, in which they specialised. They created much competition in resource trading. It was a great opportunity to increase their wealth and position in the trade market. Different resources were exported, which gave the Phoenicians a good profit margin.

INNOVATION:

The Phoenicians embraced many innovations. The use of sails and other navigation instruments helped them increase their economy. This helped them increase their competitiveness in the market. It increased their maritime capabilities, which benefited them much in the future.

All these strategies collectively helped them remain competitive. It helped them prosper in the evolving markets of their time. They also greatly emphasised market research and adapted to the local market demands.

The Phoenicians diversified into new markets. This was their key strategy in expanding their business. They achieve diversification through the following strategies:

- They extended their trade routes to North Africa, Cyprus, Spain, Sicily, etc.

- They started founding colonies, which helped them in trading more efficiently. These colonies helped them in trading in the market.

- They also adapted to available local resources. This includes timber from Mediterranean forests. It helps in enhancing their ability to engage in diverse trade.

- They made brilliant trade networks, which helped them transport goods more efficiently to various locations.

By diversifying in new markets, they expanded their trade. It also increased their influence, making them a strong force in Mediterranean trade

networks.

HARNESSING TECHNOLOGY FOR BUSINESS GROWTH

The Phoenicians harnessed technology for their business growth. They maintain their prominence in the trade industry. Following are some of the ways through which they have utilised technology in increasing their business growth.

They are very well-known shipbuilders. So, they have developed an advanced range of vessels with amazing designs. They use different selling mechanisms, navigation instruments, and steering mechanisms to increase the cargo capacity. This helps them in increasing the trade and making it more efficient. It helps them in trading across long distances very easily.

They developed navigation instruments as well. It helped them in reaching distant markets very easily. These navigation tools include celestial observations, astrolabs and compasses. All these navigation instruments were helpful in sea trade. The navigation instruments ensure their business growth as well.

The Phoenicians also had great expertise in metallurgy. They produced valuable metal goods. All the goods that were in demand in different nearby and distant markets were produced by them. Then, they traded those metal products and earned a good revenue.

They also introduced many sophisticated techniques for Purple dry production. They extracted purple dye from snails in the sea. This technology was very helpful in producing highly valuable luxury items. It multiplied their economy and trade in different regions.

Phoenicians have also adopted many advanced water management techniques. All these techniques helped support and provide sustainability in their business.

By implementing all the techniques and advancements in the business sector, they have ensured they gain more profit and efficiency in their trade operations. These technologies contributed to the continued success and prominence of the Phoenicians in the ancient world.

Modern businesses also use technology from the ancient world because it helped them advance and provide success in their business. Like the formations, they have also harnessed technology to enhance their operations and competitiveness in the market.

Strategies for increasing their business growth.

Modern businesses have also implemented many strategies. They utilise a huge advanced technology change to improve efficiency and reach wider markets. All these strategies and innovations are like how Phoenicians hardened the technology to grow trade in the ancient world.

The modern business of e-commerce and Logistics uses automation and artificial intelligence-driven inventory management to increase their sales. This streamlined management can be done using the ancient world's technology. Many manufacturers of 3D printing have a printing technology that creates customised products. It also reduces the production cost and gives them high profits. Printing technology was also developed by Phoenicians, which is helpful for modern businesses.

Different companies use various energy-efficient technologies to produce renewable energy. This is a concept that has arrived from the past. It reduces environmental impact and reduces the cost of energy.

MARKET RESEARCH AND INNOVATION

The Phoenicians practised a lot to make their name in the trade market. They have introduced many technologies and innovative products that have extended their market growth. The Phoenicians used different methods of exchange during trade. They traded goods through different methods. High-quality and luxurious goods were exchanged with other reciprocal gifts. The goods were also exchanged through the barter system. The prices and quantities of these goods were fixed before they made any agreement during trade. These were all techniques and strategies made efficiently by the Phoenicians to remove any risk and loss.

They produce a large variety of crops. This was because their irrigation system was strong and was developed by them to produce a large variety of crops. They were also known as the best wood exporters. This was because they had forests in the region.

Using raw materials, they also exported textiles, including silk, wool, linen, and cotton. The Phoenicians converted them into colourful products. These products include carpets, curtains, clothes, etc. Also, they had produced clothes from the Purple dye extracted from the sea snails. These purple-dyed clothes were used and gained much fame in the ancient world.

The Phoenicians were also included in the import of different goods. These goods include copper, silver, iron, and gold. These raw materials were imported and transformed into great ornaments and vessels. Then those products were exported with a good profit. They also imported ivory from India. It was used in making artificial jewellery. Embroidered linen was also imported, which was used in making cloths. These clothes were exported at good prices.

THE TYRIAN PURPLE REVOLUTION

The innovative discovery of Tyrian Purple in the city of Tyre is a great mystery. The Tyrian purple is also called Imperial purple or Royal purple. It was a very luxurious dye used to create different luxurious ornaments. It was extracted from sea snails that were found in the Mediterranean Sea. Many people say that the Tyrian Purple Discovery was accidental. It was seen that on the beach, a dog bites a sea Snail and then gets its mouth stained purple. At that time, the people of Tyre discovered this Tyrian purple dye. The discovery of this dye was the secret among the financial people.

This purple dye was produced by extracting the dye from many snails. Many small snails were used and crushed in the production of this dye. Then, they were fermented in the sunlight, transforming the liquid into a purple dye. But the exact method is still a secret of the ancient times. This Tyrian purple became a symbol of prestige in ancient times. It was very luxurious and of incredible cost at that time.

This time, purple dye was used to dye the clothes of Royal people and emperors. As the dye came into the market, the demand for it increased. It increased the economy of Tyre and significantly resulted in the enhancement of wealth in the Mediterranean region. It changed the condition of Tyre City and left a very indelible mark on history. It became a symbol of status, pride, and luxury for centuries.

The Tyrian Purple Revolution increased the business of Phoenicians. It increased the wealth and trade in the Mediterranean sector. The Phoenicians had a monopoly on the Tyrian Purple production. Its extraction process was intensive and required much labour and knowledge. This is why it is a very prestigious and rare dye. It was well known for its vibrant colour and ability to become brighter in sunlight. In various ancient civilisations, this purple dye was in great demand from royals. The kings and emperors of different civilisations used Tyrian Purple to signify their wealth and status.

Due to its huge demand and rarity, it was very valuable. The Phoenicians could charge high prices for this dye, making it more profitable in trade. They also traded Tyrian Purple with other goods, which enhanced their overall trade business.

SUMMARY

The Phoenicians were well known for their significant contributions to trade and innovation in the ancient Mediterranean. They were exceptional sailors and shipbuilders. Also, they were known for their robust and high-performance ships. They were involved in the production of valuable goods. These goods include textiles, dyes (including the famous Tyrian purple dye), glassware, and metals.

The Phoenicians played a very important role in shaping the ancient Mediterranean world. This was done through their maritime success, extensive trade networks, invention of the alphabet, production of valuable goods, and contributions to navigation.

The Phoenicians became famous for their innovative techniques. They were well known for Maritime trade and the communication systems that they developed to stay relevant. Following the spirit of continuous innovation can also be valuable for modern businesses. You must keep exploring new technologies and innovations in today's constantly changing world. Innovative ideas and strategies should exist to adapt and succeed in the changing environment.

Chapter. **6**

THE SPIRIT OF EXPLORATION

We all know that exploration is a natural human urge that has driven advancement and discovery throughout history. Adventure enthusiasts push beyond boundaries, following in the footsteps of ancient Phoenician navigators and courageous astronauts mapping the oceans and reaching for the stars. The Phoenicians, with an inventive spirit and a keen sense of exploration, transcendently contributed to the development of global commerce, consequently shaping civilisation. By studying Phoenician expeditions, we may embrace adventurous exploration, tolerate scientific risks, and discover the unidentified in a vigorous maritime world.

The Phoenicians in the maritime industry paved the way for exploration, which resulted in significant benefits to their industry. No historical explorations can match those made by the Phoenicians.

This chapter's discussion centres around Phoenician explorations and their influence on global knowledge. Apart from covering risk management and its influence on nautical exploration, we will also delve into the rich history of the Phoenicians.

PHOENICIAN EXPLORATION: PIONEERS OF THE SEA

The Phoenicians, also regarded as pioneers of the sea, were a remarkable seafaring civilisation that emerged around 3,000 BCE in the coastal Levantine region of the eastern Mediterranean. As skilled shipbuilders and navigators, they realised the abundant opportunities awaiting them beyond their narrow homeland. The Phoenicians thus developed a thriving maritime trade network that expanded their influence across the Mediterranean and beyond.

If we talk about Phoenician civilisation, intensive maritime commerce became the pillar of that civilisation. Their strategic coastal cities, such as Tyre, Sidon, and Byblos, housed advanced shipyards, and bustling harbours brimming with goods from Phoenician forests provided the raw material for their sturdy, agile ships capable of remarkable voyages.

The Phoenicians also honed vital navigational skills using the stars, sun, and prevailing winds to venture far into uncharted waters. Their maritime mastery and pioneering spirit transformed Phoenician cities into dominant commercial powers in the ancient world.

Around 3,000 BCE, in the coastal Levantine region of the eastern Mediterranean, the Phoenicians emerged as pioneers of the sea and, notably, seafaring civilisations. Skilled shipbuilders and navigators they discovered the wealth of possibilities lying outside their limited homeland. The Phoenicians saw their power grow as they formed a successful shipping network that stretched far into the Mediterranean and beyond. Intensive maritime commerce supported the Phoenician civilisation. These coastal strongholds, such as Tyre, Sidon, and Byblos, had well-established shipyards that produced nimble ships made from the resources gathered in Phoenician forests. Their fleet ventured far due to their skilful construction.

As a result of their mastery of navigation skills, the Phoenicians could venture deep into unknown waters using the stars, sun, and prevailing winds. Their expertise in seafaring and innovation enabled Phoenician cities to become leading commercial forces in the ancient world.

EXPLORING SOME KEY EXPEDITIONS AND DISCOVERIES OF THE PHOENICIANS

EXPLORATION OF THE MEDITERRANEAN

The Phoenicians, having set sail from their native land along the coasts of present-day Lebanon and Israel, created a vast network of settlements at different points around the Mediterranean. They spread west to Cyprus, Crete, Sicily, Sardinia, Malta, and farther beyond the Strait of Gibraltar into the North African coast. These strategic outposts strengthened Phoenician dominance over important maritime routes and access to essential metals, notably silver, copper, and tin.

BEYOND THE PILLARS OF HERCULES

Enthusiasm for exploration pushed the Phoenicians even further beyond the known world. Their most daring achievement is sailing past the "Pillars of Hercules" beyond the Strait of Gibraltar. In the Mediterranean Sea, the pillars of Hercules looked like old "No Entry" signs. In the Strait of Gibraltar, they marked a tight entrance point. In those times, sailors believed that the vast Atlantic Ocean lay past these columns and into uncharted territories. It represented the outer limits of the known universe for them. The Phoenicians stunningly crossed the perils of the narrow Strait of Gibraltar past the Pillars of Hercules, forever marking their place in maritime history. Venturing down the Atlantic coast of Africa, their ships sought gold, treasures, and new markets.

ESTABLISHMENT OF TRADE ROUTES

Above all, economic incentives primarily encouraged the Phoenicians to venture forth on their expeditions. Throughout their expansion, they established a vast, interconnected oceanic trade system between major ancient civilisations.

The Mediterranean saw many Phoenician crafts when loaded with cedar wood and other items like embroidered textiles, glassware, and pottery. Having travelled far distances for prosperous trade agreements abroad with amicable traders who possess exceptional resources only found within different realms than what we call "home" amidst unfamiliar landscape yearning essence adorned heavily guarded strongholds passing secrets between neighbours en route. However, always cautious against potential threats wanting nothing more than a spoil characteristic towards eminent wealth, none might know how cherished each moment held for those worthy adventurers venturing beyond. The massive scale of this maritime commerce secured Phoenician pre-eminence in the region for centuries.

CULTURAL EXCHANGE AND GLOBAL KNOWLEDGE IMPACTS OF EXPLORATION

To explore an unknown area, the Phoenicians built strong wooden boats. The ships we talked about were known as galleys, and they had rowers and sails in their design. These helped the Phoenicians navigate the rough seas during that period.

The reason the Phoenicians crossed oceans was not mere curiosity. The main goal of the trip was to exchange goods, items, and precious resources.

Encountering new territory led them to multiple countries like Spain, America, and Lebanon in the modern day. They established colonies all along the Spanish shoreline. North Africa was reached, and even further, across the Atlantic Ocean.

These daring explorations greatly influenced global knowledge in addition to trade. The largest and most impactful result was accessing key, basic geographic facts. Calling them comparable in their day to Google Maps is not wrong. They played a significant role in learning about the world through exploration, discovery, and establishment of new coastlines. The worldwide information is useful for expected findings like those of Christopher Columbus. In addition to significantly contributing to navigation and geography skills, the Phoenicians collected important information on winds and ocean currents.

The Phoenicians served to open doors for empires during that time. Hungry for exploration and trade growth, the Phoenicians ventured into diverse lands. Over time, economic power drove the development of these cities, which grew in wealth and impact on the world stage.

The Phoenicians' adventurous exploration voyages sparked lasting intellectual effects on ancient civilisations. Bold exploration unlocked vital information on cartography and navigation. In the face of their hazardous travels, Phoenician sailors kept records and navigational tools to aid the next expedition. With this, seafarers discovered a way to navigate far in the open sea.

But it was also the case that the Phoenicians innovated significant navigational methods. To find latitude, they made a calculation based on the locations of celestial objects. These ships voyaged near North Africa's shore with the leverage of prevailing eastern breezes before returning home on western oceanic currents, understanding the key to navigating tidal winds decades earlier than Western Europeans. Geographical, navigational, and meteorological understanding progressed as such innovations spread across the Mediterranean region.

Another result of Phoenician exploration was the cross-cultural transmission of ideas and knowledge. Interacting with multiple cultures at the time, these traders had a significant impact on knowledge. Not only did they return with antiquities, but they also opened the door to cross-cultural information exchange. They were incorporating different ideas related to various cultures. This intercultural experience had a meaningful effect on the ancient world, leading to a deeper understanding and greater awareness of diverse cultures.

The Phoenicians also had another important contribution to make. Is it your belief that the Phoenicians were the first to uncover the alphabet you are learning? Yes, you heard correctly. The Phoenicians used pictures or symbols to represent the sounds of their language a long time ago to express their ideas. Later, symbols and images were transformed into simpler ones to understand and remember. Currently, the word "Phoenician alphabets" applies to these condensed characters.

THE STUDY OF PHOENICIAN EXPLORATION TO BENEFIT CURRENT SAILORS AND SHIPBUILDERS

Essential lessons for contemporary shipping industry success can be found in the entrepreneurial spirit of Phoenician seafarers, who navigated our fast-changing world with a sense of adventure.

FOSTERING A SPIRIT OF EXPLORATION

By driving Phoenician expeditions into unknown realms with a spirit of exploration, the present-day traders must foster curiosity, wonder, and a hunger for discovery within themselves. Modern maritime enterprises owe their success to pushing boundaries as front-runners, ever so driven by the spirit of exploration. Keep the adventurous spirit that drives human progress within reach.

To the Phoenicians, enormous ocean areas not yet mapped were seen as opportunities for development instead of sources of scarcity or avoidance through courage and skill. To tackle the present obstacles within their industry, integrating concepts from this old lesson would be helpful for modern maritime leaders.

DISCOVERING NEW MARKETS

The Phoenicians' relentless explorations targeted new regions brimming with raw materials, goods, and markets ripe for exploitation through trade. Likewise, identifying untapped opportunities and pioneering access to new markets provides a competitive edge.

Due to their small Levantine homeland, the Phoenicians could only partially rely on local markets but were forced to range widely across the Mediterranean. This expansion allowed them to dominate maritime trade.

EMBRACING INNOVATIVE ROUTES

The Phoenicians remained commercially dominant by embracing advances in shipbuilding and navigation, from sails to celestial navigation. Likewise, today's maritime sector must adapt nimbly to changing technological and market realities to avoid being left adrift. Keep abreast of breakthrough innovations, from digitalisation, automation, and AI to advances in ship fuels.

The Phoenicians' mastery of shipbuilding and navigation was key to their success.

Invest in state-of-the-art navigational systems, stronger and smarter material designs, and cleaner propulsion. A spirit of bold exploration means venturing confidently on the cutting edge of progress.

The Phoenicians ventured across diverse lands, seeking raw materials and thriving markets ripe for trade to be harnessed through commerce. A key factor in staying ahead of the competition is identifying untapped opportunities and breaking into new markets.

EMBRACING INNOVATIVE ROUTES

The Phoenicians stayed preeminent in commerce by adopting innovations in shipbuilding and navigation, including sails and celestial navigation. Able to adapt quickly, the modern maritime field must adjust to evolving technology and markets to stay relevant.

Stay upbeat about pioneering new ideas by monitoring progress on all levels, from cutting-edge technologies like artificial intelligence (AI) and computer automation through more traditional areas, such as improved transport flux via better ship fuel systems! The Phoenicians' mastery of crafting and navigating ships enabled them to thrive.

Consider investing in state-of-the-art navigational systems, smarter material designs, and cleaner propulsion choices. Bold exploration is venturing confidently on the cutting edge of progress.

EMBRACING THE UNKNOWN WITH RISK MANAGEMENT

The daring voyages of the Phoenicians give an educational example of careful risk management when venturing through challenging seas that are not well known.

CALCULATED RISK-TAKING

It is without a doubt that Phoenician expansion needed courage when embarking on long, perilous voyages into unmapped territories. While highly irresponsible, their actions were not the result of carefree whims. Risks and potential benefits were weighed against one another.

Today, maritime ventures confront decision-makers with complex trade-offs between opportunity and prudent caution. Rewards exist outside protected harbours, so take courage and embrace the challenges. Make sure risks are deliberately weighed and managed through preparation rather than recklessly taken. They honed their nautical skills through the triumphs and tragedies of past voyages. Just as past risk scenarios can teach maritime organisations today, they can also learn from similar situations.

PREPARING FOR THE UNKNOWN

Navigating uncharted waters guided only by courage, skill, and celestial observations, Phoenician sailors braved mysterious seas past the Pillars of Hercules. Navigational tools help, but sailors venture into uncharted seas while shipping goods.

Address potential problems by preparing contingency plans and emergency response capabilities for situations arising from piracy, extreme weather episodes, or other unanticipated threats during maritime activities. Dare to lead, but brace for rough sailing.

Despite their extraordinary abilities, Phoenician vessels faced the perils of storms and pirate attacks. Even on routine voyages in well-travelled waters, advanced planning and crisis response capabilities are essential safeguards. In case of crew injuries or onboard fires, ensure comprehensive contingency plans and drills are ready. Select strong ships with well-trained crew members and reliable ways to communicate.

PHOENICIAN EXPLORATION: REAL LIFE IN PRACTICE
The Journey of Hanno the Explorer

A 5th-century BCE explorer, Hanno, offers one of the most detailed accounts of Phoenicia's intrepid voyages.

With a fleet of 60 ships carrying 30,000 sailors and colonists, Hanno journeyed into the tropics, though exact dates remain uncertain. His expedition travelled along the South African coast for many months, setting up ports and exploring uncharted territory new to the Phoenicians.

Hanno described unfamiliar oceanic regions inhabited by exotic wildlife, from sharks to gorillas to volcanic mountains that erupted in flames. He also records his encounters with hostile local tribes that opposed Phoenician sailing vessels on their shores. Hanno's account paints a fascinating picture of the expanding past.

Carthage began as a Phoenician colony, eventually becoming a major Mediterranean naval power. Located across the Strait of Gibraltar, Gadir provided the Phoenicians with a foothold in the Atlantic, minerals, and access to new markets. These cities stimulated Phoenician trade through cultural dissemination and exchange.

The Phoenician settlement also had a profound effect on their adopted lands.

The Phoenician heritage of intercultural exchange laid the foundation for the transnational customs of the future Mediterranean world. Their early colonies were vessels that fostered close ties and influenced economic development at the local level.

THE LEGACY OF THE PHOENIX RESEARCH

The nautical knowledge accumulated by the Phoenician voyages had a lasting impact on future explorers. Greece and Rome embraced their trading Phoenician civilisation routes. At the same time, navigation and chart navigation developments inspired mediaeval navigators and later European explorers such as Columbus and the legacy Phoenicia offered in shipping and trade.

Through the sea phenomena, the Phoenicians inspired humanity's view of the world as infinite and connected. They pioneered open ocean shipping and trade and set the stage for our modern mixed global economy. Their heroic heritage inspires fascinating expeditions to new frontiers long after their ancient civilisations have disappeared.

SUMMARY

This is a vast unknown outside their native shores, where the Phoenicians saw opportunity, not danger. As maritime pioneers, their courage and vision changed people's minds through exploration. Their innovations and remarkable efficiency led to extensive maritime trading systems that linked ancient cultures through trade. Embracing a spirit of fearless exploration, the Phoenicians opened the transformative power of navigation and trade.

The incredible achievements of the ancient Phoenicians hold invaluable insights for maritime leaders charting the waters of today's dynamic global economy. By nurturing balanced courage and prudent preparation, seeking new opportunities globally, and embracing the latest developments as pioneers, today's shipyards can live up to the phoenix spirit of pioneering when the object to be found is encountered.

The sky is still endlessly stretched out before us and full of possibilities. Like those brave Phoenician voyagers who ventured into the unknown behind the pillars of Hercules, nautical guides today can choose new paths that can enhance human knowledge and well-being through a spirit of curious exploration, embrace change in air atoms, and move forward with confidence.

Chapter 7

UPHOLDING BUSINESS ETHICS

usiness ethics are more than just a set of rules. They constitute the essence that moulds a business's character within the commercial realm, defined by one or more moral values. However, it is unfortunate that there is no specific case study to provide insight into the Phoenicians' business ethics and the precise code of conduct that steered their trade endeavours.

But on the bright side, based on the data we've gathered regarding the Phoenicians and their business practices, it's safe to assert that they fostered a business culture deeply rooted in ethical principles. It's evident that there's no successful business without trust, and trust is built upon honesty and moral values. With the seven principles of business ethics in mind, we will shed light in this chapter on the Phoenicians' remarkable commitment to ethical commerce.

PHOENICIAN ETHICAL PRINCIPLES IN TRADE AND COMMERCE

A. Fair Trade Practices

It is evident from many documents that the Phoenicians never used coins. Their entire business relied on the barter system, which can be tricky because it's hard to determine the value of two things. However, the Phoenicians proudly conducted their trade successfully using this system.

Why? Because of their fair-trade practices. The Phoenicians were very conscientious in their dealings and ensured that their buyers received goods of equal value to what they gave. For example, they often give their customers several gifts to acquire one item. This remarkable approach prevented exploitation and ensured fair exchanges, which was the hallmark of Phoenician traders.

B. Honesty and Integrity

Merchants dealt with various expensive goods, from silk to spices, timber to precious jewels. It's also evident that these products were not all produced or mined in one place. This meant that Phoenicians had to constantly travel to faraway lands to acquire goods from one place to another.

It's also apparent that the dealers were familiar with the Phoenicians. That's because no one wanted to sell high-quality and expensive goods like silk, wine, and jewels to fraudsters. The Phoenicians built the foundation of their business relationships on honesty and integrity.

Furthermore, it's evident that they rarely lied or haggled for cheap goods in their dealings.

Although there are no documents mentioning them dealing with low-quality items to deceive their clients. However, the slogan of honesty and integrity is applied in many businesses today. Inspired by these ancient mariners, modern businesses should understand that transparency in dealings can help retain customers' trust, leading to more business.

Thus, we can reasonably assume that the Phoenicians earned their well-deserved reputation as honourable merchants. This sterling reputation attracted other merchants eager to engage in business with them and granted the Phoenicians the remarkable endurance to thrive in commerce for nearly a millennium.

C. Quality Assurance

As mentioned earlier, nearly all the items the Phoenicians were bartering for were expensive and hard-to-obtain goods. This included wine, silk, precious metals, timber, and, most notably, Tyrian purple dye, an exceptionally expensive and rare item of that time. It was so costly that purple became associated with royalty due to its high price.

If you're a dealer of costly merchandise, you must guarantee the impeccable quality of the goods you handle. After all, can you imagine any discerning individual, especially royalty, settling for anything less than top-notch products? Ensuring absolute quality stands as their foremost priority.

As we've determined, the ingenious Phoenicians first championed delivering unrivalled value through superior products. Today's businesses have wholeheartedly embraced this philosophy. Although a market still exists for cheap and copied goods, true success is reserved for those who painstakingly ensure that the quality of their products unequivocally justifies their price.

THE IMPORTANCE OF ETHICS IN BUILDING TRUST AND SUSTAINABLE PARTNERSHIPS

Now, it's time to delve into the importance of business in the context of fostering trust within and outside the organisation. We must remember that trust can be established through strong components such as fairness, honesty, and respect for others' opinions and rights.

A. Trust as a Cornerstone

It is the cornerstone in realising the dream of maintaining a successful, healthy, and sustainable business environment. Trust here doesn't solely refer to the trust between customers and merchants. Instead, our primary focus should be building an organisation where workers can trust their employers because they dedicate their time and effort to the cause. Conversely, employers should trust their employees with the projects they are tasked with, as they involve the company's financial investments.

In the same way, when an organisation cultivates a healthy environment built on trust, it paves the way for a successful business. In this regard, there are valuable lessons to be learned from the Phoenicians. It wasn't merely their time that their ship workers dedicated; they risked their own lives for their cause.

For instance, picture yourself embarking on a voyage with your employer into an uncharted world, facing unknown hazards in the open sea. This demands immense trust between the Phoenician ship workers and their employers to undertake such risks. Similarly, the ship owner or the one who funded the voyage also had to trust their sailors to navigate successfully, thus ensuring the business's triumphant success.

Therefore, trust within the organisation can pave the path to a successful business. When devoted, employees tend to produce high-quality products, which fosters positive dealings. Similarly, in the Phoenician era, establishing trust from one merchant to another was crucial. During a time when legal frameworks were not as developed, reliance rested largely on verbal agreements. This meant that one had to place considerable trust in promises made through word of mouth.

Believing in such agreements required a great deal of faith. Consequently, we can surmise that the Phoenicians were masters at maintaining trust, allowing them to build a mighty trading empire solely on the foundation of verbal commitments.

B. Sustainability and Reputation

All the principles of business ethics collectively contribute to a business's sustainability and reputation within its industry. As the name implies, goodwill plays a pivotal role in attracting more leads to a business. This goodwill is nurtured through the application of honesty, the offering of valuable products, and the establishment of trust in business practices.

Furthermore, companies that adhere to business ethics are adept at averting legal and financial complications. In the modern era, businesses have elevated these principles to new heights. Charity events have become common facets of business ethics today.

In conclusion, regardless of the scale, businesses should pay attention to the fundamental essence of business ethics exemplified by the Phoenicians. They didn't feign transparency; they genuinely demonstrated it to their customers, a timeless lesson for all.

SUMMARY

In summary, the Phoenicians impart numerous valuable business ethics lessons, from delivering high-quality products to nurturing trusting word-of-mouth relationships. By treading the path laid out by the Phoenicians, we ensure the sustainability of our business success and find satisfaction in providing value to our customers and earning their enduring loyalty.

THE FINAL NOTE

No matter the field, from the marvellous shipbuilders to the brilliant traders, Phoenicians have left their mark on history with precise business acumen and an eye for detail. There's no doubt there are many lessons that modern businesspeople, sailors, and shipbuilders can learn from despite living in an advanced world. Their remarkable shipbuilding skills helped them navigate the deep sea and discover new lands, leading to the discovery and innovation of superior goods. Later, these superior goods made the Phoenicians brilliant and wealthy traders.

They invented, discovered, explored, and succeeded, leaving no proof of failure. Also, their adaptation to other cultures, which we didn't often see in ancient times, helped them establish commercial colonies and map out new trades. Their success in trade also proves that they researched their market and planned on time, all while ensuring the delivery of high-quality products with a high calibre of business ethics.

However, it's truly unfortunate that we lack sufficient data about the fate of the civilisation. Yet, on the brighter side, we have tangible evidence of their remarkable lessons in history. Let us not forget that neglecting these ancient civilisations serves us no purpose. Instead, let's wholeheartedly embrace these lessons and elevate modern shipbuilding and trading techniques, seeking new trade horizons, fostering business growth through sea routes, and championing the global fusion of cultures, just as the Phoenicians did.

FINAL SUMMARY

Ships were a popular feature for centuries, and the same remains true today. However, there was an era of inventors and seafarers from the Levant region *(The Eastern Mediterranean region of West Asia)* who left behind a plethora of knowledge called the Phoenicians. Several of their concepts continue to inspire new-aged sea traders, mariners and sailors.

Given their expertise in building merchant ships and sailor boats, they also developed the "trireme", the most revered warship of their time. A noteworthy fact is that they were open in the sense that they didn't believe in the superiority of their own culture, and they were always willing to adapt to increase knowledge and boost trading options.

The Phoenicians were the first civilisation to develop a maritime trading network and establish several monopolies across a vast empire, including three continents. Their expertise was also evident in their port management skills in terms of more room to carry cargo and efficient unloading and collection of goods. Although much is still to be discovered about the Phoenicians, the records in various shipwrecks speak volumes of their trading and engineering prowess.